Exploring Down Under
An Australian Geography Journey for Kids

Exploring Down Under: An Australian Geography Journey for Kids

© 2024

By Michelle Morrow

Contributions by Belinda Letchford and Anna Marsh

Illustrations: Michelle Morrow, Tim Morrow and Sarah Graham

Paperback edition

ISBN: 978-1-7635287-4-1

Published by My Homeschool PTY LTD

NSW, Australia

Authors Note: Portions of this book have been republished and updated from *Discover Downunder*, originally published in 2013.

This book is copyright. It is not for individual sale. Apart from any fair dealing for the purposes of private study, research, criticism or review as permitted under the Copyright Act, no part may be reproduced, stored in a retrieval system, or transmitted, in any form or by any means, electronic, mechanical, photocopying, recording or otherwise without prior permission.

All enquiries to My Homeschool PTY LTD

https://myhomeschool.com

Table of Contents

To Parents...4

1. Exploring Australia 9
2. On Country 13
3. Defining Australia 17
4. New South Wales 22
5. Australian Capital Territory 30
6. Victoria..36
7. Tasmania...42
8. South Australia 49
9. Western Australia 54
10. Northern Territory...59
11. Queensland 65
12. Australian External Territories.....................73
13. Our Neighbours – Indonesia 79
14. Our Neighbours – Papua New Guinea 85
15. Our Neighbours – South Pacific 92
16. Our Neighbours – New Zealand......................97

To Parents

'Most of us have gone through a good deal of drudgery in the way of 'geography' lessons, but how much do we remember? Just the pleasant bits we heard from travelled friends, about the Rhine, or Paris, or Venice, or bits from The Voyages of Captain Cook, or other pleasant tales of travel and adventure.' Charlotte Mason

Geography can be a very interesting subject for children. It is much more than a fact finding expedition. It can be done in a way that will capture a child's interest and give them a sense of adventure as they get to know the lay of the land.

When I first began homeschooling there were no good geography books in print that were suitable for young students. What I wanted was a simple narrative overview of Australia. Eventually I decided one needed to be written. Most of the stories are from my travels and experiences across Australia and neighbouring countries, but we also have some special contributions from Belinda Letchford who wrote about her home state of Western Australia and Anna Marsh who wrote about her time living in the Northern Territory.

This resource is an overview of the states and territories of Australia and our neighbouring countries. It's written as a personal narrative and uses Charlotte Mason's panoramic method.

'The panoramic method unrolls the landscape of the world, region by region, before the eyes of the scholar within every region its own conditions of climate, its productions, its people, their industries and their history. This way of teaching the most delightful of all subjects has the effect of giving to a map of a country or region the brilliancy of colour and the wealth of detail which a panorama might afford, together with a sense of proportion and a knowledge of general principles.' Charlotte Mason

How to Extend the Lessons

This book can be read on its own or you can use it as the springboard for further study. Here are some suggestions.

1. Read the selected chapter.

2. Ask your child to tell you what they learnt after reading the chapter.

3. Complete the *Discovery Activities* at the end of the chapter.

4. Begin a travel journal of your own. Encourage an oral narration from the child about the chapter and discuss any local knowledge your family may have that

relate to the content. For example, have they been to any of the places mentioned in that chapter. Have them write a few sentences about each state in their own words.

5. Add a local study. When you are studying your own region do further investigations, adding photographs, local events, newspaper clippings, transport options, and information about the community.

See if you can compare the past and present pictures of your community. These may be present at a library.

Discuss the physical geography. Are there any wetlands, nature reserves, mountain ranges, recreation parks?

Look for local indigenous history and discover the Aboriginal language group associated with your region.

6. Use a map to look up the location of the place being studied. There are some maps in this book, but they are not drawn to scale. Use your own Australia map, an atlas, or online map, as a reference to find the major landmarks discussed in each chapter.

'…geography should be learned chiefly from maps. Pictorial readings and talks introduce him to the subject, but as soon as his geography lessons become definite, they are to be learned, in the first place, from the map.' Charlotte Mason

We hope you will enjoy learning about Australia through the eyes of our authors.

Happy Homeschooling!

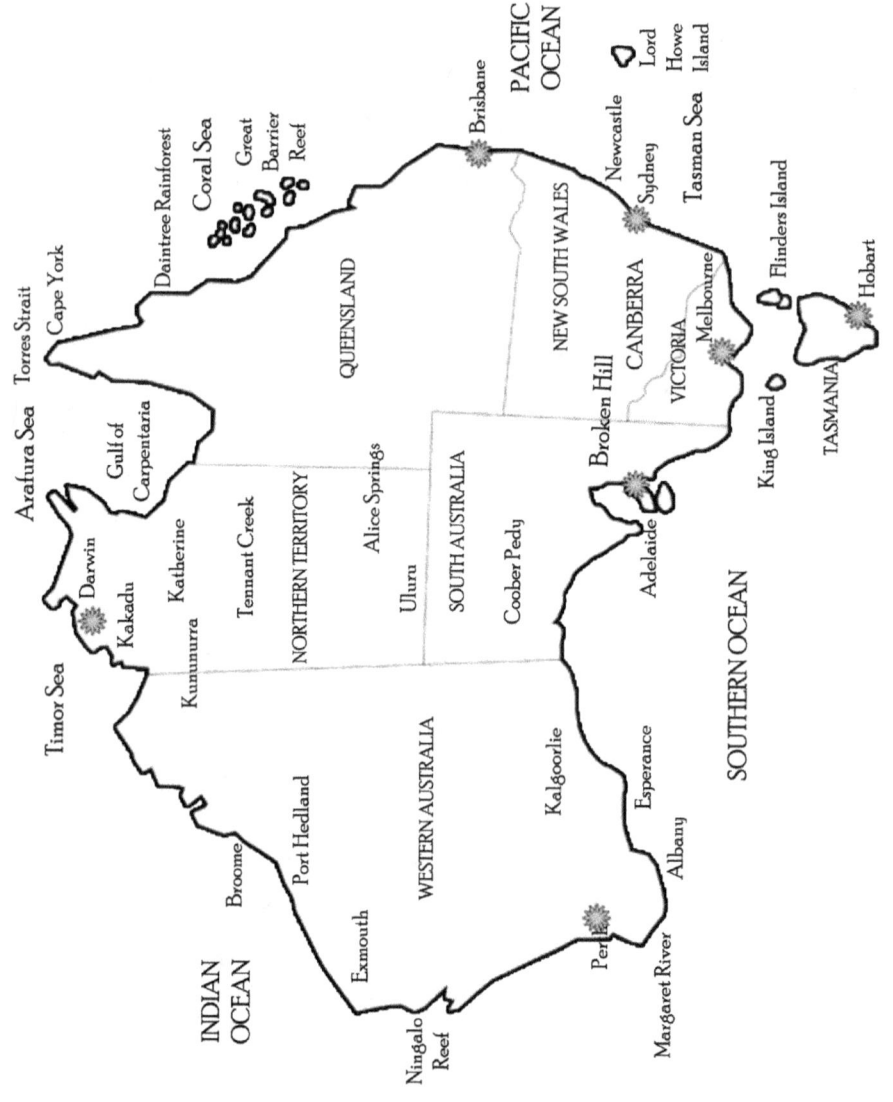

1. Exploring Australia

My Grandma lived near Melbourne, and we lived in Sydney. She had an English accent and told stories of England and, for much of my childhood, I thought Melbourne was in England. In my teenage years I was surprised to find out that Melbourne was actually in Australia, and part of Victoria! Part of the reason I never worked out where Melbourne was had something to do with the fact I wasn't taught much about geography at school and maps didn't interest me.

Now I know so much more about the geography of Australia. It's the smallest continent but the sixth biggest country; the mainland is the world's biggest island. There are 8,222 islands within its maritime borders. It lies in the southern hemisphere, and it's surrounded by three oceans, therefore it shares no land borders with the neighbouring countries of Papua New Guinea, Indonesia, South Pacific Islands and New Zealand.

It is the world's driest inhabited place with ten deserts. Six different time zones operate in the country: Australian Eastern time, Australian Central time, Australian Western time, Norfolk Island time, Lord Howe time and Christmas Island time. There are even more if you include daylight savings. There are six states, two mainland territories and nine external territories. Our longest river is the Murray River. Our highest mountain is Mount Kosciuszko. The capital of Australia is Canberra and Australia's population is over twenty-six million people.

So, you can see how very great and big Australia is. There is the Great Barrier Reef, Great Artesian Basin, Great Dividing Range, Great Australian Bight, Great Victorian Desert, Great Sandy Desert, and the Great Ocean Road. Our mainland has the big rock—Uluru, the biggest salt-lake, the biggest coal port, the biggest fence, and the biggest group of feral camels. We have even made our own big tourist attractions like the Big Banana in NSW, Big Pineapple in Queensland, and Big Lobster in South Australia—just to name a few. And one of the very great big things about Australia is how diverse the geography is. Tropical rainforests, hot sandy deserts, alpine snow fields, temperate coastal cities, underground towns, and wildflower wonderlands are all found in this one country, Australia.

Although many of the recorded explorations, naming, and mapping were done by early English explorers less than two hundred and fifty years ago, many things had already been named and discovered by the indigenous Aboriginal people that had lived here long before the

English convict settlements began. The Aborigines worked out: the seasons, where to go for water, what to eat in different places, and how to track animals. Their tradition of moving from place to place meant that they didn't really need towns or villages as we now have but they did have special meeting places and special celebrations and names for these places. Today we are returning to some of these Aboriginal names and recognising the significance that these places have to particular indigenous peoples. That is why some places have two names, an aboriginal one and the commonly known name.

Australia's geography is unique, and this book will explain some of its distinctive features in more detail.

Most of the illustrations are by Tim and Sarah, my kids who learnt about Australia's geography while we prepared this book. Map illustrations have been created for this book; they are not drawn to scale, and some are artistic impressions.

I hope you enjoy Exploring Down Under.

Discovery Activities

1. Tell what you have learnt this lesson.

2. What is the population of Australia?

3. Which is the biggest state in land size? Which is the smallest state in land size?

4. Find these places on a map:

- Victoria
- Tasmania
- Canberra
- Queensland
- South Australia
- New South Wales
- Western Australia
- Northern Territory

2. On Country

Have you ever looked at an Aboriginal painting with bright coloured dots, swirling tracks and brilliant animals? Have you ever seen a traditional Aboriginal dance or heard an Aboriginal song? Did you ever think that these may have been maps? Well, they may have been. The Aboriginal people have used pictures, songs and dance to tell about Australia long before it was known by that name. These maps, drawn, sung and danced may describe special places for the Aboriginal people: places where they meet with another clan, places where they might go for a corroboree, places where only men can go, places where only women can go. They might even tell you what direction you should go, and where you should go next. Some of these maps are shared with non-Aboriginals but some of this geography is kept a secret and only shared between Aboriginal clans.

In a time before machinery, mining, farming, cities, and technology, the Aboriginal and Torres Strait Islanders lived in Australia. They had a close connection with the land. They learnt how to treat the land and how to manage it. This country is where their heritage is. It is the place of their ancestors and for them the country is their home, their history, their land and part of them. It's not just a place on a map.

Aboriginals and Torres Strait Islanders think of the geography of Australia quite differently from the clear surveyed boundaries of states and territories. Their borders are made according to their languages, clans and traditions. An Indigenous Australia map is like a vibrant patchwork. There are about two hundred and fifty multicoloured shapes filling the map and each of these different shapes represents a unique group of people with their own language, stories, and traditions. These divisions are called 'traditional geopolitical borders'. They aren't lines on a map like we use today, but they are just as important for the Aboriginal people. This map helps us understand and celebrate the rich and diverse cultures that have been a part of Australia for thousands of years.

Today, the Australian Government law recognises some of these traditional boundaries and land rights. And the diversity of cultures gives us clues to how the Aboriginal people and Torres Strait Islanders see this country. They look to their traditional laws to understand the land, its history and ownership.

Australians sometimes call this country the 'Lucky Country' because it is blessed with natural resources, food in abundance, rugged beauty, modern cities, modern transport and wealth for many. However, it is not just luck that will keep this country a beautiful place to live. A key lies with understanding what the Aboriginal people and Torres Strait Islanders already know. It is the knowledge that this country is more than just land. It is a home for plants and animals and the many people who call themselves Australian.

'Welcome to Country' and the 'Acknowledgement of Country' are two ways Australian people acknowledge that Aboriginal Australians were the traditional inhabitants of Australia before the British Settlement of 1788.

During a 'Welcome to Country', an Aboriginal person from the local area might do a special ceremony. They might tell stories, sing songs, or perform dances that have been passed down through generations. It's a way to share their culture and history with everyone who has come to visit, learn, or celebrate on their land.

Australians often begin meetings and gatherings with a saying called an 'Acknowledgment of Country.' It usually goes like this: 'We acknowledge the Traditional Owners of the land on which we meet today and pay our respects to their Elders, past and present.' It's a way of saying we understand and appreciate their history, culture, and their special connection to the land.

So, when you hear 'Welcome to Country' or an 'Acknowledgement of Country' in Australia, it's a mark of respect and acknowledgment of the importance of the land to the Aboriginal people.

Discovery Activities

1. Look up the Indigenous Australia map online.

https://aiatsis.gov.au/explore/map-indigenous-australia

2. What Aboriginal language is your region known for?

3. Defining Australia

Australia is a vast and diverse land, and it's important to have good maps to help us understand and explore it. Maps are like a special code that tells us about the country and how it all fits together. But Australia's mapping story isn't just about lines and shapes; it's also a journey through time, cultures, and stories.

Australia is defined by its borders. This is an imaginary line separating one region of land or territory from another. A geopolitical border is more about people agreeing on these lines—for example, where Australia ends, and Papua New Guinea begins. As a nation, Australia has no land borders. It shares maritime borders with East Timor, Indonesia, New Zealand, Papua New Guinea, Solomon Islands, and the islands of New Caledonia.

Now, let's dive into how Australia's geopolitical maps work. I'm sure you've seen these maps before and seen how they show you the states and territories of Australia. But did you know that Australia is divided into six states and two territories? These are like different puzzle pieces that make up the whole country.

The states are New South Wales, Victoria, Queensland,

South Australia, Western Australia, and Tasmania. The two territories are the Australian Capital Territory (ACT), where our capital city Canberra is, and the Northern Territory. Each of these states and territories has its own special characteristics, like animals, landscapes, and even sports teams.

Australia is also a country with lots of diverse landscapes, from sandy deserts to lush rainforests. Maps help us understand where these different places are. For instance, the famous Uluru is in the Northern Territory, and it's a massive red rock in the desert. It's sacred to the local Aboriginal people.

Maps also show us where cities and towns are located. Sydney, Melbourne, Brisbane, and Perth are some of the biggest cities. But there are also lots of smaller towns all over the country, each with its own story to tell.

A topographical border is different again; it's made by nature, like a big river or a line of mountains that can also show where one place stops, and another starts. It's like how a fence or a hedge in your garden shows where different parts are, except it's made by nature, not people!

If you look at a topographical map of Australia, you'll notice a series of lines, bumps, and colours on the east side. These show the Great Dividing Range, a huge line of mountains and hills that stretch from Queensland, down through New South Wales, and all the way to Victoria. It looks like a big, wavy adventure trail, telling us where the land rises into tall mountains and where it dips down into little valleys. When you follow these lines with your finger, you can imagine how water flows down from these mountains to create rivers, and how the mountains are like guardians, watching over the cities, farms, and forests below.

The Murray–Darling River is the longest river in the country. Most of the rivers in the Murray–Darling Basin start in the Great Dividing Range. The Basin is divided into two parts, northern waters run into the Darling River and water in the south runs into the Murray River.

Murray-Darling River and Tributaries

So, Australia's maps aren't just about lines and shapes; they're a way for us to learn about history, culture, landscapes and creatures that make Australia so special. They help us appreciate the traditions of the Indigenous people and the diverse communities that have come together to create the nation we know today.

Next time you look at a map of Australia, remember that it's not just a piece of paper; it's a window to the incredible stories and adventures that make up our great land. And who knows, one day you might even explore some of these places and create your own stories to add to Australia's rich history.

Isn't it amazing how a map can turn into a story about Australia?

Discovery Activities

1. Tell what you have learnt this lesson.

2. Find these places on a map:

- East Timor
- Indonesia
- Papua New Guinea
- New Zealand
- Antarctica
- Indian Ocean

- Timor Sea
- Arafura Sea
- Coral Sea
- Pacific Ocean
- Tasman Sea
- Fiji, Vanuatu, New Caledonia

4. New South Wales

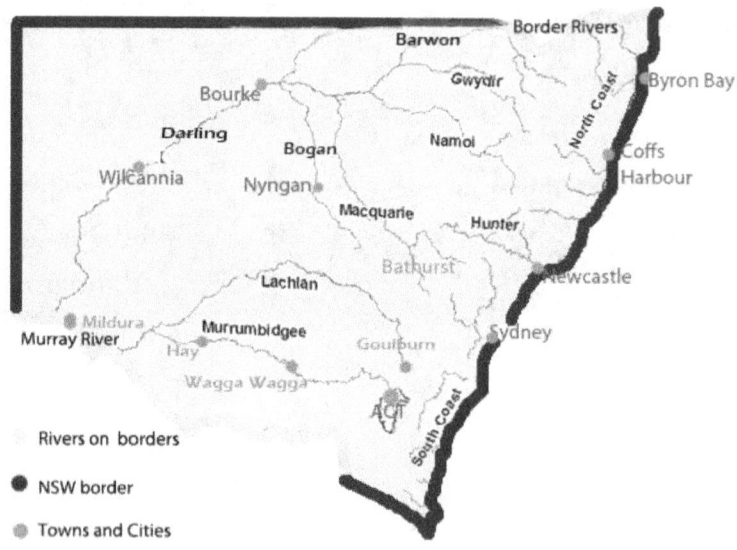

New South Wales (NSW) was the name given to the whole of the east coast of Australia by the British explorer Captain Cook in 1770. A few years later, in 1788, Captain Phillip hoisted a flag at Sydney Cove and Australia's first British settlement was born. British men began exploring and mapping the coastlines and rivers. For the next forty years no particular borders were set but then as new colonies sprouted, boundary lines were drawn; and in 1901 at Federation the borders were set. Whilst still the largest populated state, NSW's size has shrunk to only 10% of Australia's land mass. Over eight million people live in NSW, and more than five million of them live in its capital Sydney. At least three quarters of the population live along the coast.

The twin towns of Coolangatta and Tweed Heads are where Queensland and NSW's coastal border is found. From an aerial view you can see a road that stretches across the outback dividing NSW from Queensland. Here you will find two deserts and one city. Cameron's Corner in the Strzelecki Desert, a sandy dune desert, is the border point between NSW, Queensland and South Australia. Broken Hill is the most remote city in NSW. It is Australia's oldest mining town, with a colonial history dating back to the 1880's, and is in the South Australian time zone.

The Murray River defines most of the wiggly Victorian border until it reaches the South Australian border just before Renmark.

To drive from Tweed Heads to Albury and Wodonga, the twin towns on the Victorian—NSW border, would take you 14 hours non-stop. It's 1366 kilometres. On your trip, seaside holiday destinations dot the coastal border of NSW. The subtropical weather of Byron Bay means it is holiday season in the north all year. Cape Byron, an hour's drive south from the Queensland border, is the most eastern tip of the Australian mainland. Further south, driving through Coffs Harbour, you'll see the Big Banana, a tourist attraction and cafe, built in 1960's to celebrate the region's banana production. Today, whilst still growing bananas, Coffs Harbour also provides more than 50% of the nation's blueberries.

Tamworth and Gunnedah, in the Liverpool Plains, are inland from the coast, but east of the Warrumbungle Ranges. They are considered to have some of the richest fertile soils in Australia.

Moving further southward it becomes cooler, but the summers are still sunny and hot. Bondi, in Sydney, is Australia's most famous beach, however there are many other NSW beaches that are much more beautiful.

The Hunter region is one of the country's best-known and most-visited wine regions, thanks to its easy drive from Sydney. There are also 41 coal mines operating in the Hunter and most of them are open cut mines. As you fly over the region you will see the vineyards, but you will also see big chunks of land carved out by heavy machinery. Most of the coal is exported and the port of Newcastle is one of the biggest coal ports in the world with more than 1400 ships coming to collect coal for Japan, South Korea, Taiwan, and India. Newcastle is the next largest city in NSW.

Sydney, the capital city of NSW, is known for its Opera House and the Harbour Bridge. It is also often included high on the list of most popular world cities. It has become famous for its fireworks display on New Year's Eve, with one billion people watching around the world as spectacular fireworks say goodbye to one year and welcome in the next.

South of Sydney, you'll find Wollongong, the third most populated NSW city, it is also a coal port. At Kiama there is a blowhole that can shoot water out of its spout up to 60 metres in the air, making it one of the highest in the world.

Coastal rainfall is high, and many short rivers drain into the Pacific Ocean along the coast.

In the Southern Highlands the climate is cool, even in summer. The Blue Mountains in the Central Tablelands are a tourist attraction and a World Heritage area, two hours west of Sydney. This national park has the Three Sisters (a well-known rock formation), majestic gorges, bush walks, and the scenic railway. Wollemi Pines, a rare tree species dating back to the time of the dinosaurs, were discovered here and their location is kept top secret in order to protect this unique species. A little further over the mountains, and down a twisting narrow road you come to the Jenolan Caves, one of the most spectacular limestone cave systems in the world.

Mount Kosciuszko is the highest point of NSW, and Australia. It is also part of The Great Dividing Range that stretches up and down NSW. The Snowy Mountains Hydroelectricity scheme, located here as the name suggests, is a civil engineering wonder that supplies electricity to NSW, Canberra and Victoria. It diverts the headwaters from the rivers and streams in the Snowy Mountains and releases them into the Murray and Murrumbidgee Rivers. As part of its construction, two townships, Jindabyne and Adaminaby, were relocated and the old towns were flooded and now lie under the stored water's surface. Thredbo and Perisher are the two largest ski resorts in Kosciuszko National Park. The ski season usually lasts from June to early October.

Over the Great Dividing Range it is mostly flat land or gentle slopes and it's divided into two main regions. The first is the agricultural region of Wagga Wagga and the Riverina districts. Within this region the Murrumbidgee River, Lachlan River and Murray River are all found, so water supply is good for irrigated farming. The Western Plains is the other region. It is also part of the Murray-Darling Basin, but the water supply is not secure, and the area is drought-prone, even though its soil is fertile. Regional communities still attract tourists with country shows, Parkes Observatory, which assisted in the Apollo 11 Moon Landing in 1969, and the Western Plains Zoo.

In the outback, beyond Wilcannia and Bourke, you can visit White Cliffs in NSW, a place so remote and tucked away, people often say it's 'out the back of Bourke' or in 'whoop-whoop' – that's Aussie slang for being in the middle of nowhere! This tiny, fascinating town is famous for its dazzling opal mines and something super cool – an underground hotel! In White Cliffs, the sun blazes hot overhead, turning the landscape into a sea of shimmering heat. So, people have dug homes and even a hotel right into the cool, comforting earth. Staying in this underground hotel is like exploring a hidden cave, with cosy rooms carved out of the rock, where the walls tell tales of the land and its history. I stayed there once and what surprised me was that Barramundi was the dinner special, not your traditional outback tucker. This place isn't just a spot on a map; it's an adventure in the Australian outback, where you'll find unique treasures both above and below the ground.

Lord Howe Island, which is also a part of NSW, is a remote and picturesque island in the Tasman Sea, 600 kilometres east of Port Macquarie. It's a stunning holiday destination with pristine beaches and coral reefs. Around 360 people live there permanently, and they have a long and intriguing Christian history that dates back to the early 19th century, when European colonists and missionaries first began to colonise the area. Due to the island's historical and religious significance and the keeping of the Sabbath, a trip to Lord Howe Island on a Sunday is often regarded as a time for rest, reflection, and worship. Cars on Lord Howe Island are few in number, and mainly serve essential purposes. Walking, bikes and golf carts are the way most people get around. This approach helps to reduce traffic congestion, noise, and pollution on the island, promoting a more eco-friendly and serene environment.

One last special feature of NSW is that within its borders lies the Australian Capital Territory.

Discovery Activities

1. Tell what you have learnt this lesson.

2. Find these places on a map:

- Sydney
- Katoomba
- Mount Kosciuszko
- Broken Hill
- Bathurst
- Wagga Wagga
- Tamworth
- Byron Bay
- Cameron's Corner
- Albury—Wodonga
- Coolangatta—Tweed Heads

3. Find these rivers on a map.

- Murray River: from the Snowy Mountains along the Victorian border to South Australia.
- Murrumbidgee River: from the ACT through Wagga Wagga then Hay. It meets with the Murray River, just south of Mildura.
- Darling River: from Queensland to Bourke through Wilcannia. It joins the Murray west of Mildura.
- Barwon River: from Queensland's Border Rivers Region it joins the Darling River east of Bourke.

5. Australian Capital Territory

When Australia was a young nation, its people faced a big decision – choosing a capital city. You see, both Sydney and Melbourne were large, important cities, and each hoped to be the capital. To solve this rivalry, leaders decided to create a new city. This new city would be a symbol of unity and not belong to any state, so it wouldn't favour one over another. In 1908, they chose a peaceful area with rolling hills called Canberra, which in the local Ngunnawal people's language means 'meeting place.' It was a perfect spot, almost halfway between Sydney and Melbourne, and its design was decided through an international competition won by an American architect, Walter Burley Griffin, and his wife, Marion Mahony Griffin, in 1912.

Canberra's design was very special. It wasn't just about streets and buildings; it was about creating a city in harmony with the landscape. The Griffins imagined a city that blended nature and civilisation, with wide streets, plenty of green spaces, and beautiful buildings arranged around a big, artificial lake—named Lake Burley Griffin to honour the architects. Building the city was a huge task, and it officially became the capital in 1927 when the Parliament House was opened. Today,

Canberra is not only the political heart of Australia but also a place full of history, culture, and nature, where people from all over Australia and the world come to visit and learn about Australia's unique journey.

I've been to Canberra many times and when you first arrive in the Australian Capital Territory it has the familiar suburban sprawl that makes it feel like any other Australian City. But then as you go to the city centre there are many buildings that tell the story of how Australia became a nation.

Old Parliament House stands as a silent reminder to Australia's political evolution. This iconic building, which is now a museum, housed the nation's parliament from 1927 to 1988, and it is a testament to the growth of Australia as a self-governing nation. Walking through its corridors, you feel the echoes of past debates, the resonance of historic decisions. In the chambers where legislation had been fiercely debated, I imagine the struggles and triumphs that had shaped modern Australia.

And then there is New Parliament House, an architectural masterpiece that embodied the

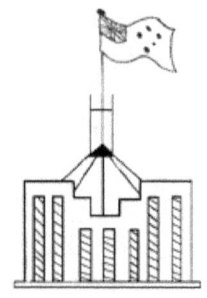

contemporary aspirations of the nation. Designed by Romaldo Giurgola, it was opened in 1988, marking a symbolic shift from the old ways to new possibilities. The impressive flagpole and the vast marble foyer strike a sense of national pride. Here you can stand at the heart of Australian democracy, gazing up at the magnificent 81-metre flagpole soaring high into the sky. It's like a beacon of the nation's values and aspirations.

Inside the building, you look to see if you can spot a politician you've seen before, or maybe a foreign diplomat. Then you can go and look at the Upper House (Senate) in its calming eucalyptus green and the Lower House (House of Representatives) in muted rose, each having their distinct functions.

An original version of the Magna Carta is housed here. This historical document is famous around the world because it embodies the ideas of constitutional and parliamentary governance.

The next place to visit is the Australian War Memorial, a place of reflection and remembrance. The memorial is a shrine to the brave men and women who sacrificed their lives in service to Australia. The Roll of Honour, an intricate and moving display of names, is a reminder of the profound cost of conflict. As I explored the museum, I was drawn into the stories of courage and sacrifice. The dioramas and exhibits vividly recounted Australia's involvement in wars, from Gallipoli to more recent conflicts. It was a humbling experience, reminding me of the importance of peace and the debt of gratitude we owe to those who have given their all.

The Tomb of the Unknown Soldier at the Australian War Memorial is a place of profound significance, representing the sacrifice and service of all those who have served in Australia's defence forces. The tomb itself is a sacred site, holding the unidentified remains of an Australian soldier who gave his life during World War I. The tomb, a simple stone sarcophagus, serves as a symbolic resting place for all Australian servicemen and women whose names are known only to the nation they served.

The view from the Australian War Memorial to Parliament House in Canberra is not merely a geographical connection but a carefully planned architectural and town planning masterpiece that symbolises the nation's history and democratic values. This vista, known as the 'Anzac Parade,' stretches 4.5

kilometres, visually linking these two significant institutions.

The next fascinating place to visit is the Royal Australian Mint. This is where all the Australian coins are made. Here, you can learn about the history of currency in Australia, from the first European settlers who used a hodgepodge of coins to the introduction of the Australian dollar—currency notes are now printed in Victoria. The mint itself is a marvel of modern technology, where coins are crafted with precision. You can watch the coin-making process, from the melting of metal to the striking of coins, and if you want you can leave with a shiny souvenir.

The city is nestled between Lake Burley Griffin and the surrounding hills, creating a breathtaking landscape that showcases the harmony between man-made and natural beauty. Wandering through the streets of Canberra, you are struck by the abundance of green spaces and public art. The city is a testament to the idea of creating a capital that was not only functional but also aesthetically pleasing.

Canberra has a four-season climate. Heat and dryness, often above 30°C (86°F), increases the risk of bushfires in summer. Autumn in Canberra is a stunning show of colour as deciduous trees drop their leaves against clear blue skies and cooler temperatures. The city becomes a winter wonderland with intermittent frosts and occasional snowfall. Spring brings the flowers and Canberra hosts a huge flower and entertainment festival called Floriade.

There is much to do when you visit Canberra. It's a journey through time and a celebration of Australian democracy and heritage. From the grandeur of New Parliament House to the solemnity of the Australian War Memorial and the intricate workings of the Royal Australian Mint, each stop tells a different aspect of Australia's story. Visiting Canberra is a trip of history and progress. You'll leave with a deeper appreciation for the nation's past and its promising future.

Discovery Activities

1. Tell what you have learnt this lesson.

2. Find Canberra on a map.

3. Research the making of Canberra.

6. Victoria

Fresh water! That's what the group of pioneering settlers were looking for in 1835 when they set up a small camp near the Yarra River in Port Phillip Bay. The small settlement of Melbourne grew slowly until the gold rush in the 1850's and then rapidly expanded to become, at one point, the largest city in Australia. Today Victoria, Australia's smallest state in land mass has Australia's second largest population and Melbourne, the capital, is the second largest city. Weather is notoriously fickle in Melbourne but in other parts the weather is similar to NSW with its temperate climate, arid patches, temperate rainforest regions and alpine ranges.

Exploring Down Under

Port Phillip Bay is more than a home for Melburnians, it is a densely populated area and where most of Victoria's population live. Mornington Peninsula on the south-eastern tip of the bay is a popular holiday destination with surf and sheltered beaches, farms, wineries and arts and crafts. On the western side of the bay the city of Geelong resides. This is a manufacturing town that is known for making many things and it's Victoria's second largest city.

Moving west along the coast you come to the Great Ocean Road. You can drive all the way to South Australia and past the famous Bells Beach, which holds the longest running surfing competition in the world. This scenic drive is filled with spectacular scenery such as the Twelve Apostles, a group of eight (not twelve) limestone rock stacks sitting close to shore in the Southern Ocean.

Moving inland from the coast you come to the Goldfields region of Ballarat and Bendigo. These are the boom towns that grew rapidly when gold was first discovered in the 1850's. Gold mining still occurs in this region.

Remnants of the gold rush can still be seen in the architecture of these towns and if you want to experience what life was like in those days you can visit the tourist theme park of Sovereign Hill in Ballarat. Moving westward it's sheep and agricultural country and continuing north towards the southern banks of the Murray River and the border of NSW we come to Mildura. And if you like sultanas then chances are they may come from this area as nearly 70% of Australia's sultanas are grown in this river region.

Following the Murray eastward to its source we end up in the Uplands, in the Great Dividing Range. Its highest point, Mount Bogong, in the Victorian Alps, is a place where Bogong Moths migrate to in summer and it's also Victoria's highest mountain. Ski resorts in this region are popular, getting a good fall of snow each winter.

East of the ranges, where the Snowy River drains into the Tasman Sea you find the Gippsland region. This is farming and coal mining land. Wilson's Promontory is the southernmost point of Australia's mainland and it's a little further along the coast. As you move back towards Port Phillip Bay you come to Phillip Island, a nature park. And at dusk each night you can see the fairy penguins march on to the beach as they bed down for the evening in their sand dune burrows.

Travelling inland again we come to the Dandenong Ranges. Toot! Toot! 'All aboard,' the conductor calls as tourists from all over the world rush into a carriage on the Puffing Billy steam train. The trip takes you through fern gullies, temperate rainforests and rolling hills. Tall Mountain Ash trees line the tracks and this is where much of the timber was collected to be used to help build Melbourne.

Back down the ranges and into the Yarra Valley to a place which inspired some of Australia's great artists at Heidelberg. The Yarra River leads us back to Melbourne and Australia's largest and busiest cargo port, Port Melbourne. From here you can embark on a thrilling boat journey across the Bass Strait, the maritime border between Victoria and Tasmania.

Imagine Melbourne's bustling cityscape with towering skyscrapers gradually disappearing behind you, while the Spirit of Tasmania, a mighty ship, cuts through the waves across the Bass Strait, a body of water known for its turbulent seas and changeable weather conditions. Many boats have been shipwrecked on this journey.

However, your sea voyage is filled with fresh, salty sea air and playful seagulls soaring over the rolling waves.

Around 10 hours later, you arrive at the Esplanade in East Devonport, on Tasmania's welcoming northern shores.

Discovery Activities

1. Tell what you have learnt this lesson.

2. Find these places on a map:

- Melbourne
- Mildura
- Bendigo
- Geelong
- Ballarat
- Phillip Island
- Snowy Mountains
- Wilsons Promontory

3. Find these rivers on a map:

- Snowy River: from the Snowy Mountains to the Tasman Sea.
- Goulburn River: from the Australian Alps to the Murray River. It crosses the NSW border at Echuca.
- Yarra River: from the Yarra Ranges east of Melbourne to Port Phillip Bay Melbourne.
- Glenelg River: from the Grampian region in south-western Victoria to the Great Australian Bight at Nelson, near the South Australian border.

7. Tasmania

In the heart of the Australian summer, I went with friends on an unforgettable trip to Tasmania. We flew into and began our adventure in Hobart, the charming capital of this island state. As we stepped off the plane, a summer's day welcomed us, but I was instantly aware of the temperature drop from the hot Sydney weather I had left only two hours before. Summers are cool by Australian standards with the average temperature between 17 and 23°C. Winters are usually between 3 and 11°C.

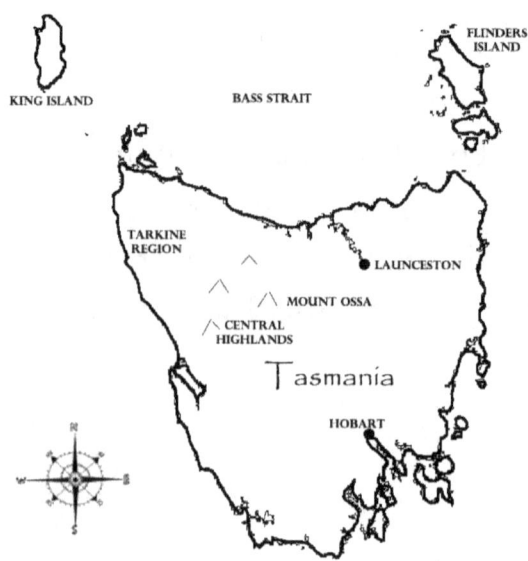

Our first few nights were in Hobart. This historic city with its sandstone buildings, has a deep connection to its colonial past. We explored the bustling Salamanca Market, indulging in local delicacies and handmade crafts.

From Hobart, we found ourselves along the Franklin River. We cruised the pristine waters, and they whispered tales of resilience, reminding us of the importance of preserving the natural world for generations to come. As we went along some turbulent rapids I decided to enjoy the ups and down of the boat. This was a mistake. I fell, biting my lip and wacking my chin. I sat down for the rest of the trip.

Our next stop was Queenstown in the West Coast of Tasmania. It is colder than other regions of Tasmania, receiving more snow and rain. This area is known for its untamed beauty. You can also go trout fishing here, but we didn't have time for that. This region echoes of a long-gone mining boom of early Tasmania.

I was there in the 1980's when there was a big conservation battle raging because they were planning to make a hydro-electricity dam on the Franklin River. This project ultimately failed because of conservationist protests. This led to one fifth of Tasmania becoming protected as a Tasmanian Wilderness World Heritage area.

These World Heritage areas also contain remnants of artifacts from the Aboriginal people who lived there prior to the British fighting and forcing them from their land. The true numbers are not known, but it has been estimated that the population of Aboriginal Palawa people was around 4,000, possibly more. Truganini (1812–1876) and Fanny Cochrane Smith (1834–1905), are considered to have been the last Aboriginal people solely of Tasmanian descent.

While there we saw much of the island's flora and fauna. Tasmania is famous for its ancient forests. Towering eucalyptus trees, such as the giant blue gum, stand tall and majestic, providing shelter to a variety of wildlife. The lush rainforests boast tree ferns, myrtle, and moss-covered logs, creating an enchanting, mystical feeling. Tasmania's stunning wildflowers, like the vibrant waratah and the delicate orchids, add colour to the landscape, especially during the spring and summer seasons.

Tasmania is also home to an incredible array of unique animal species. The iconic Tasmanian devil, a small carnivorous marsupial, is a symbol of the island and is known for its fierce personality. In addition to the devils, wallabies and pademelons (they look like tiny kangaroos) which can be spotted in the bush, there is also the mystery of the Tasmanian tiger, who is considered extinct despite occasional claims of sightings, which continues to captivate the imagination. The state's numerous rivers and lakes provide habitat for the elusive platypus (an egg-laying mammal), and its peaceful waters host a variety of bird species like the native wedge-tailed eagle and the cheeky little penguins that parade along Tasmania's shores. These diverse flora and fauna make Tasmania a treasure trove of natural wonders waiting to be explored and appreciated.

We travelled further north-west towards Cradle Mountain, a striking wilderness that has enchanted explorers and trekkers for generations. In the heart of Cradle Mountain—Lake St Clair National Park, we were greeted by the vivid greenery of summer but we were told sometimes it can still snow in summer! The tranquil Dove Lake, mirroring the surrounding peaks, felt magical and reminded us of the ancient natural forces at play here. The park's history was rife with tales of early settlers and intrepid bushwalkers, their endeavours etched into the very landscape we crossed.

From Cradle Mountain we drove to Devonport, where the Spirit of Tasmania arrives from Melbourne after sailing across the Bass Strait. Two more significant islands belonging to Tasmania are also located in the Bass Strait: King Island known for its outstanding dairy produce and the tallest lighthouse in the Southern hemisphere, and Flinders Island, an 8 hour ferry trip from Bridport. Despite being home to only 800 people, tourists often visit Flinders Island to enjoy hiking and the natural beauty.

Launceston, Tasmania's second largest city, nestled in Tasmania's north, was the next place to visit. The summer here was a picture of lush gardens and Victorian-era architecture. Cataract Gorge, with its suspension bridge and peacocks strolling in the sunshine, offered a serene retreat, in stark contrast to the tumultuous rapids that have carved this natural wonder over the centuries. Launceston's historical charm was evident as we explored its elegant streets, reflecting the legacy of its early European settlers.

From Launceston we drove another 3 hours to Port

Arthur. This former convict colony on the Tasman Peninsula mesmerised us with its historical significance and sombre beauty. As we explored the well-preserved ruins and listened to the eerie tales of hardship and hope, we were transported to an era when this isolated settlement served as a prison.

We finish our trip in Hobart and are ready to go back home. We are leaving by plane to Sydney, but we discover Hobart acts as a departure point for the Antarctic as well. Scientists and tourists board ice-strengthened vessels at Macquarie Wharf to depart on voyages that allow them to witness and study the Antarctic's breathtaking landscapes and wildlife which is one of Earth's most pristine and remote wilderness areas.

Discovery Activities

1. Tell what you have learnt this lesson.

2. Find these places on a map:

- Hobart
- Queenstown
- Bass Strait
- Devonport
- Launceston
- Cradle Mountain
- King Island
- Flinders Island

3. Find these rivers on a map:

- Mersey River: from Cradle Mountain, towards Devonport and into Bass Strait.
- Tamar River: from Launceston to Bass Strait.
- Derwent River: from Lake St Clair to the Port of Hobart.
- Huon River: from Lake Pedder to Cygnet Bay and the Tasman Sea.
- Franklin/Gordon Rivers which are a part of the Wild Rivers area west of Hobart.

8. South Australia

If you were to look up facts about South Australia probably the first one you would find would be that it is the driest state. Then you might find out how it is bordered by all the mainland states and the Northern Territory. After that, you might note that 7% of Australia's population live in this state and the capital city is Adelaide. Those facts make South Australia sound pretty boring and don't really tell you much at all about this diverse and beautiful part of Australia.

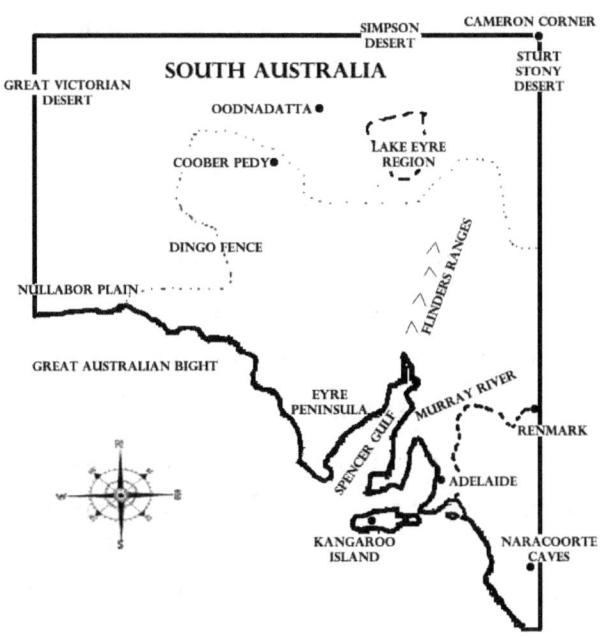

When Adelaide was founded along the banks of the Torrens River, its city streets were defined in a grid  pattern, and in its early days it was called the City of Churches for it had many. Today several of these churches have been knocked down to make way for a more modern city. Close to the city there are the Adelaide Hills, a picturesque place with botanic gardens, farms and vineyards. Naracoorte Caves is an underground limestone treasure close to the Victorian border. This World Heritage site has many megafauna fossils.

Paddle steamers meander along the mighty Murray River as it winds its way out towards the Southern Ocean. These tourist boats were once the transport system used from New South Wales and Victoria to South Australia and back. This river, no longer a water highway, is still a vital part of South Australia's agricultural economy, delivering irrigation to many wineries and farms and supplying drinking water to 90% of South Australians.

South Australia's coastline with its high cliffs and pristine beaches was first mapped by Matthew Flinders, the

British explorer. The Eyre Peninsula, South Australia's commercial fishing hub, is enclosed by Spencer Gulf to the east and the Great Australian Bight to the west. Flinders also mapped and named Kangaroo Island which you can visit by a short ferry ride from the mainland. A community of fewer than 5000 people continue to farm the land but it also provides a haven for many endangered Australian native animals. Visiting here is said to be like visiting a zoo without fences. Kangaroos hop about, sea lions and penguins rest in safety, koalas gobble gum leaves and echidnas plod along unafraid of a human's presence. This pocket of South Australia, from the Victorian border in the south-eastern corner along the coast of Adelaide and the Eyre Peninsula and out to the Adelaide Hills, is mostly a well-watered temperate climate with warm summers and wet winters. And along this section of coast is where nearly all South Australians live.

From this pocket of South Australia you stretch out toward the outback where the climate is desert-like but not without its beauty. The Flinders Ranges is where the outback begins in South Australia. In amongst these vast red rock hills the animals of the desert thrive. Further into the centre of Australia you pass the Dingo Fence, the longest fence in the world stretching 5,614 kilometres. It was built to protect farm animals from the dingoes. Now it also tries to keep out the feral camels that wander the outback. This area is sparsely populated and much of the traffic is from tourists, or road trains taking supplies to parts of central Australia.

Oodnadatta, a small outback desert town, is where Australia's highest known temperature was measured at 50.7°C. It was also the place where the Ghan train from Adelaide used to stop. Now a new track has been made and the train goes all the way to Darwin via Alice Springs and this town was bypassed. Coober Pedy is another outback town in South Australia. Like White Cliffs in NSW, it is famous for its opals and dugout homes where people live underground to protect themselves from the scorching heat.

Water in the outback is scarce but you can find hot springs from water in the Great Artesian Basin. Kati Thandra—Lake Eyre—is a dry salt bed that fills with water from flooded rivers in the north-eastern parts of Australia every few years. Amazingly, you find abundant birdlife and even fish in this temporary lake.

Of Australia's ten deserts, portions of six are found in South Australia. The Great Victoria Desert is the largest desert in Australia and has a thriving indigenous community. Separating this desert from the sea is the Nullarbor Plain, a long stretch of dry flat country which connects South Australia to Western Australia.

Discovery Activities

1. Tell what you have learnt this lesson.

2. Find these places on a map:

    - Adelaide
    - Coober Pedy
    - Eyre Peninsula
    - Flinders Ranges
    - Oodnadatta
    - Mt Gambier
    - Kangaroo Island
    - Nullarbor Plain
    - Great Victorian Desert
    - Great Australian Bight

3. Find these rivers on a map:

    - Murray River from the NSW border to just south-east of Adelaide.
    - River Torrens from the Adelaide Hills to Adelaide.
    - Lake Eyre, which is a dry lake most of the time but when it fills it is the largest Lake in Australia.

9. Western Australia

Written by Belinda Letchford

Western Australia our largest State (one-third of Australia's mass) is divided into eight regions—each with its own special land features, industry, climates and lifestyles.

The Kimberley region (where my family lives) is often seen as the 'last frontier' and it has a mixture of tourism, agriculture (cattle and food production), mining (ore, gas, and diamonds) and yet maintains an 'outback' feel. Located in the north-west of Western Australia, the three largest towns are Broome, Derby and Kununurra. Here, the rocks are red and rugged. The rivers are big and are filled yearly by monsoon rains. One of these rivers has been dammed, making the Ord River Dam. Its storage reservoir, Lake Argyle, is the largest man-made body of water in the world.

I grew up in the Pilbara; a land that is rich with iron ore. The Pilbara's main centres are the city of Karratha and the township of Port Hedland. I have fond memories of counting very long iron-ore trains, and camping out in the bush, beside dry riverbeds, with graceful white ghost gums for shade, swimming in waterholes, and enjoying a campfire breakfast before the heat of the day reached its peak. These days the Hammersley Gorge is a tourist attraction well-known for its breathtaking gorges and waterfalls, but when I was a girl it was a quiet place.

The country starts to change when you get to the Midwest. There are still rugged ranges, such as the flat-topped Moresby Ranges, and the gorges at Kalbarri, but the landscape becomes more gentle and flat as you head south. The weather also changes from the heat of the tropics to more temperate weather patterns. The longest river, the Gascoyne, fluctuates between being flooded and being dry, as do most rivers in this part of the country.

The south of this state is divided into several smaller regions. The Wheatbelt obviously grows wheat but it also contributes wool, mining, and other agricultural crops. The outstanding geological landmark in this region is Wave Rock – a wall of rock that looks like a wave about to break. The south-west region is luscious, and quite unlike the rugged gorges and deserts of the rest of the state. The giant Karri trees and underground caves are just two of the unique drawcards to this region. Albany, one of the most southern towns, was the gathering place for our ANZAC soldiers before they headed off for World War I.

The Indian Ocean wraps the spectacular coastline of Western Australia. Moving from the remote and wild coast of the Kimberley, where waterfalls seem to fall horizontally, to the World Heritage listed Shark Bay, with its incredible variety of coral and wildflowers, fish and other sea animals, and birds. Further south you have the shipwreck coastline of Western Australia—where some of our most terrible history is remembered. Then down the south tip of Western Australia you will find lighthouses, relics of the whaling industry and modern-day surfers.

One of my favourite places to drive through when I was a teenager, was Kalgoorlie—it's a modern town with a mixture of new and old buildings. I would wonder about the people who used to live there in the early days. My great grandfather travelled across Australia to find his fortune prospecting in the Kalgoorlie goldfields (but I don't think he found much!). Gold is still mined here though the technology has changed, bringing us the Superpit, the biggest open pit mine in Australia. One of the engineering feats of our early history was the pipeline (563 kilometres long) from Perth to Kalgoorlie—bringing water to the desert for the gold mining towns.

Perth, the capital of Western Australia sits on the Swan River. It's a gentle, sunny city with a casual lifestyle and yet it has maintained a modern perspective as it keeps up with the ever-expanding diversity of its state.

It's a big state—there are caves and deserts, gorges and mountains, oceans and rivers. There's gold, and ore, pink diamonds and salt—cattle, sheep and fish. There are boabs and gum trees, birds, kangaroos and quokkas. We grow wheat, grapes, mangoes and sandalwood. Each year there's a trail of wild-flowers that bloom from one end of the state to the other. Though I've lived here for many years and I've travelled many kilometres, there is much of this state that I have yet to see.

Discovery Activities

1. Tell what you have learnt this lesson.

2. Find these places on a map:

- Perth
- Albany
- Esperance
- Kalgoorlie
- Exmouth
- Geraldton
- Port Hedland
- Broome
- Kununurra
- Gibson Desert
- Great Sandy Desert

3. Find these rivers on a map:

- Swan/Avon River which supplies Perth.
- Margaret River is in the south-western corner of WA and is known for its wineries. There are two rivers with this name in WA. The other can be found in the Kimberley region. It merges with the Fitzroy River.
- Fitzroy River which passes through Fitzroy Crossing and empties near Derby.
- Gascoyne River, which is the longest river in WA.
- Ord River is found in the Kimberley region of WA. Its irrigation scheme has the largest artificial lake volume in Australia—Lake Argyle.

10. Northern Territory

Written by Anna Marsh

Recently I flew from Darwin to Sydney. As we gained altitude, I could see the land stretching out beneath me. I was fascinated by the lush greenness, and the rivers twisting their way to the coast like the writhing of a snake in an Aboriginal Dreamtime legend.

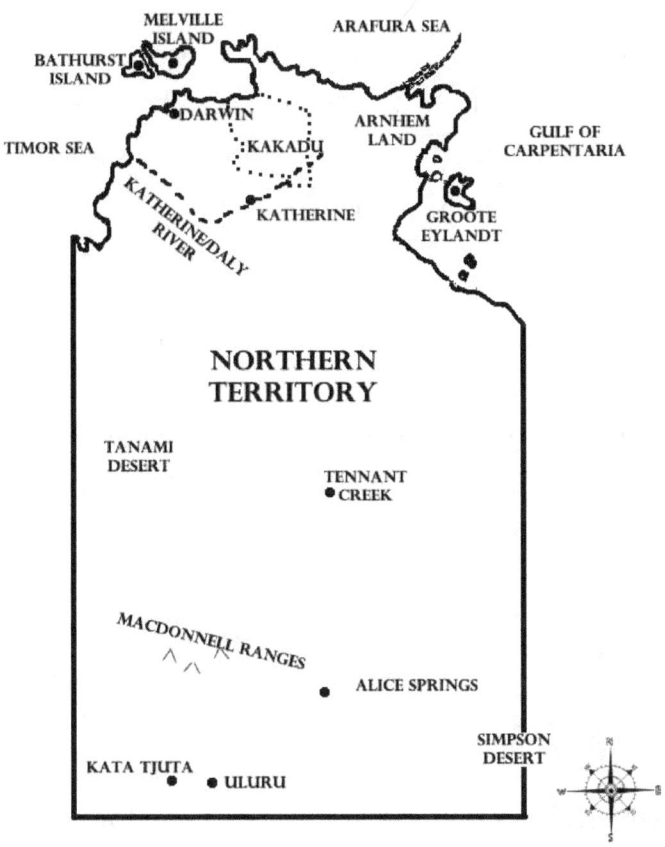

Soon I could see the sandstone ridges and cliffs of the Kakadu National Park stretching away in the distance. As the aeroplane flew southeast, the land soon changed. The dark green of the well-watered coastal plains gave way to the tree-studded brown of the more arid regions. This was cattle country. Soon the only features I could see were the patterns made by the long straight dirt tracks between the bores which provide cattle with water.

If we had gone even further south, we could have seen the rippling waves of the red brown sandhills of the Simpson Desert. This vast, arid area is about the size of Lebanon. Along with the Tanami Desert to the west, these deserts give rise to the name of 'the Red Centre' of Australia.

This is the Northern Territory, the northern central part of Australia. It is bordered by Western Australia, South Australia, and Queensland. The northern coast is washed by the Timor and Arafura Seas. There are a number of islands along the ragged coast, the largest of which are Bathurst Island, Melville Island, and Groote Eylandt.

The 'Top End', which extends from the coast south to the town of Katherine, has a tropical climate. Most people think there are two main seasons: 'The Wet', which has heavy rain and sometimes cyclones, from

December to March; and 'The Dry', with its hot, dry weather and cooler nights, from May to October. However, the local Aboriginals divide the year into five or six seasons, reflecting their more intimate understanding of the subtleties of the weather, the corresponding flowering and fruiting of plants, and the activities of wildlife. These seasonal variations can be experienced in the Kakadu National Park, with its floodplains and wetlands, stretching away to the sandstone escarpment of the plateaus, where waterfalls cascade.

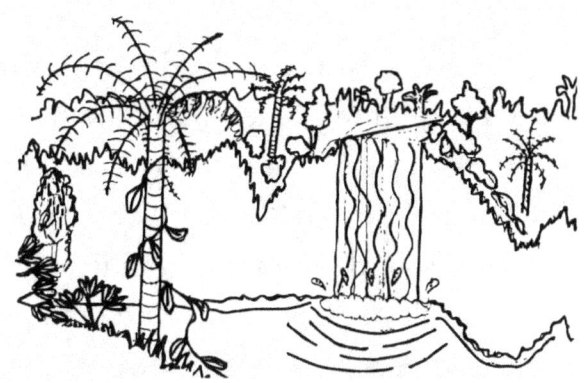

This national park is famous for its wildlife and for the many ancient Aboriginal rock paintings. Also famous is the neighbouring Nitmiluk National Park (Katherine Gorge), a series of colourful sandstone canyons carved by the Katherine/Daly River, the longest river in the Northern Territory. Then there is Arnhem Land which extends east from Kakadu to the Gulf of Carpentaria, it is an Aboriginal reserve.

The southern parts of the Territory, the arid Central Australia, experience four seasons, more like the southern states of Australia, but with little rainfall. There are few creeks and rivers. This is home to some of Australia's best known natural features. Uluru (Ayers Rock), is the world's largest exposed rock, a vibrant, red sandstone monolith that rises above the desert plains. Kata Tjuta (or The Olgas) is another famous landmark— a group of domed rock formations to the west of Uluru. This area is World Heritage listed.

Alice Springs, the town is in the middle of Australia is surrounded by the stunning MacDonnell Ranges to its east and west. Further north, near the town of Tennant Creek, are found the 'Devil's Marbles', or Karlu Karlu. These are gigantic, rounded granite boulders, some of which are spectacularly balanced, and red dirt is everywhere. The dirt gets its red colour from something called iron, which is what metal things like your bike might be made of. When the iron in the soil mixes with the air, it rusts just like metal does when it gets old and turns this beautiful red colour. It's not just pretty to look at; this red dirt tells a story about the land being very old and dry, and it's a big part of what makes areas like Alice Springs and Uluru so unique and special. Plus, when you walk on this red earth, your feet might turn a little red too, just like wearing a bit of the desert as a souvenir!

These many natural features, together with the varied wildlife, attract many tourists to this part of Australia.

The Northern Territory is the least populated of Australia's states and territories but nearly a third of the population is Aboriginal. There are smaller settlements scattered across the Territory. The larger population centres are located along the Stuart Highway (colloquially called 'the Track') which travels up the middle of the Territory, culminating in the city of Darwin, which is the capital, and the place where this journey began.

Discovery Activities

1. Tell what you have learnt this lesson.

2. Find these places on a map:

   - Darwin
   - Kakadu National Park—Jabiru
   - Katherine
   - Daly Waters
   - Tennant Creek
   - Alice Springs
   - Tanami Desert
   - Gulf of Carpentaria
   - Timor Sea
   - Uluru
   - Arnhem Land

3. Find these rivers on a map.

   - Roper River, which is slightly east from Katherine to the Gulf of Carpentaria and forms the southern border of Arnhem land.
   - Katherine/Daly River from Nitmiluk National Park (Katherine Gorge) through Katherine and northwest to the Timor Sea.
   - Victoria River, which is north of Tanami Desert and empties into the Timor Sea.
   - McArthur River from the Barkley tablelands to the Gulf of Carpentaria near Borroloola.

11. Queensland

Cape York is where a day begins with a golden ocean sunrise and ends with a pastel ocean sunset. This truly is the Top End, mainland Australia's most northerly point. However Australia's most northerly town is on Thursday Island in the Torres Strait, a thirty-eight kilometre ferry trip from Cape York. There are more than one hundred and fifty islands in the Torres Strait group and eighteen

of them are inhabited including Boigu Island, which is only six kilometres from Papua New Guinea.

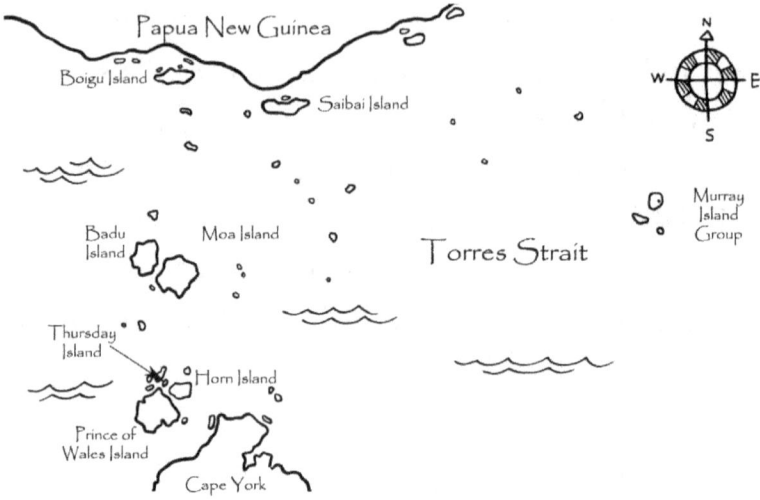

From Karumba to Cape York to Cairns lies the region of Far North Queensland. This area is surrounded by the Gulf of Carpentaria, Arafura Sea and Coral Sea. Deadly box jellyfish and salt water crocodiles share these warm waters. Wild rivers, excellent fishing, rainforests, white sandy beaches, cyclones and bauxite mining are all here. Weipa, on the western side of the cape, is the biggest town on The Gulf of Carpentaria; other Gulf communities have close family ties with this largely indigenous community. Mount Bartle Frere, in the cooler Atherton Tablelands, is Queensland's highest mountain.

Nearly half of all Australian rainforests are found in the wet tropics of the Daintree National Park. A multitude of animals can be found here including giant green frogs, the purple and blue cassowary, flying foxes, striped possums and colourful butterflies. Although a place of vast beauty, visitors need to be aware that there are also saltwater crocodiles in the rivers and snakes, ticks and leeches in the forest. At Cape Tribulation the Daintree River and Tropical Rainforest intersect with the Great Barrier Reef.

Tropical north Queensland is sheltered by the Great Barrier Reef in the Coral Sea. This reef is one of Australia's jewels. Here marine plants, coral and animals can be found in the 2900 reefs and 900 islands. Seen from outer space, this reef is the largest in the world stretching 2300 kilometres. Cairns is the largest town in the region and the tourist gateway to the World Heritage listed Great Barrier Reef and Daintree Rainforest.

As you move south down the coast of Queensland it becomes a dry tropical climate. Even the humpback whales know this is a nice place to spend winter. Around Hervey Bay and Fraser Island (another World Heritage listed site), the whales rest before journeying back to Antarctic waters. Large ships cross the reef bringing imports and collecting coal, gas and sugar from the ports of Gladstone and Townsville. Mackay has three sugar mills for the sugar cane grown nearby. The Whitsunday Islands are a perfect place for sailing or holidaying.

Theme parks, zoos and nature getaways are found on the Sunshine Coast and Gold Coast which borders NSW.

The Brisbane River winds and weaves its way through Brisbane, Queensland's capital, and empties into Moreton Bay. The city lies on a coastal floodplain and the river's source is near Toowoomba in the Darling Downs, a subtropical alpine region with four distinct seasons and lovely gardens.

Queensland rivers flood! Charleville, the Lockyer Valley, Toowoomba and even Brisbane have experienced devastating floods. The Queenslander homes built on stilts for ventilation are also a safeguard against flooding. Rain comes in the summer months and dry rivers fill and drain inland towards Cooper's Creek, part of the Lake Eyre Basin, the Murray-Darling Basin and east to the Pacific Ocean. The Flinders River is Queensland's longest river; its source is in the Great Dividing Range but it moves west and drains into the Gulf of Carpentaria.

Over the range we come to the outback, almost half Queensland's land mass. Mt Isa, a large mining town, is close to the Northern Territory border. The climate is hot and dry in summer and mild to cool in winter. The outback is mostly dry flat plains and the Great Artesian

Basin provides much of the needed water for irrigation, farming and mining.

The Great Artesian Basin is a huge, hidden underground water surprise! Imagine a giant, secret pool of water, bigger than any pool you've seen, hiding under the ground in Australia, especially under a big part of Queensland. It's like nature's own underground water tank, holding lots and lots of water that comes from rain and rivers, soaking into the ground over thousands of years. This water is really important for people, animals, and farms in places like Queensland, because sometimes it's very dry on the surface, and they need water to drink and grow food. People use special wells to get this water up from the ground, just like you might use a straw to drink from a cup, so they can use it for all sorts of things. In 1898, Thargomindah, using the bore water from the Great Artesian Basin became one of the first towns in Australia to produce hydro-electricity in Australia.

On outback cattle stations, sheep and cattle are often hand fed during drought periods, but even when it rains, and the water holes fill, the red dirt, sparse mulga shrubs, scattered native grasses, and gums make the land still looks thirsty. The Simpson Desert and the Dingo Fence are around the southwestern border shared with South Australia and New South Wales. Emus and feral camels roam wild.

The Royal Flying Doctor Service of Australia has bases in Cloncurry and Charleville. From here they offer clinics, telephone medical support and emergency air ambulances. Queensland has the most airports in Australia, and many can be found in the outback. Sometimes a plane is the only way to get around when areas are flooded. Qantas, Australia's oldest airline was first based in Queensland's outback at Winton and Longreach. Can you guess what the letters of QANTAS originally stood for? They stood for '**Q**ueensland **a**nd **N**orthern **T**erritory **A**erial **S**ervices Ltd'

Queensland is called the Sunshine State which is a very descriptive name. Do you agree?

Discovery Activities

1. Tell what you have learnt this lesson.

2. Find these places on a map:

- Brisbane
- Surfers Paradise (Gold Coast)
- Noosa (Sunshine Coast)
- Toowoomba
- Bundaberg
- Fraser Island
- Whitsunday Islands
- Townsville
- Cairns
- Cloncurry
- Birdsville
- Longreach
- Mount Isa
- Cape York

3. Find these rivers on a map:

- Balonne River and Warrego River, which both drain into the Murray-Darling River System.
- Wenlock River, which has the highest diversity of freshwater fish of all Australia's rivers. It can be found near Cape York.
- Brisbane River and its major tributaries is the longest river in south-east Queensland. The Brisbane River begins near Toowoomba, and drains into Moreton Bay Brisbane.
- Flinders River which is Queensland's longest river (1,004 kilometres). It begins west of The Great Dividing Range and drains 25 km west of Karumba.

12. Australian External Territories

In Australia's external territories, there are several islands that offer unique experiences. Some are inhabited and others are not.

Let's begin in the Indian Ocean with the Cocos (Keeling) Islands, which has a mostly Muslim population of around 600 people. Most of the permanent residents are of Malay and Chinese descent, and they have lived on the islands for generations. There are some Australian government personnel and services on the islands. Their way of life is deeply connected to the natural beauty and resources of the islands, including fishing and coconut cultivation. The local population maintains a close-knit and welcoming community on these remote coral islands. The islands also welcome visitors, particularly tourists, seeking to enjoy the stunning natural surroundings and clear waters, contributing to the local economy.

There are two known Christmas Islands, one is located in the Pacific Ocean and is part of the Republic of Kiribati. The other, the Australian Christmas Island, is situated in the Indian Ocean and is much closer to

Indonesia than mainland Australia. Its population is over 1700 people and like the Cocos Islands a significant portion of the population are Muslim of Malay and Chinese descent but there are also many other Eurasians and Australian born residents. Phosphate mining and tourism are the main sources of income. With a tropical climate, it's known for its diverse wildlife, including unique birds and iconic crabs, particularly the red crabs, which cause road closures during the wet season when millions of them migrate from the forest to the coast to breed.

The territory of the Ashmore and Cartier Islands is a group of uninhabited islands in the Indian Ocean and Timor Sea. Like Cocos and Christmas Island, they lie near the southern edge of the equatorial region. They have a tropical monsoon climate and temperatures vary little throughout the year. These islands, protected as a nature reserve, are known for their rich marine biodiversity, coral reefs and lagoons which support a variety of species.

Moving around to the Pacific Ocean we find the Coral Sea Islands Territory. This includes numerous islets and atolls located in the Coral Sea east of the Australian mainland. These uninhabited islands are known for their pristine marine environments, making them important for conservation efforts.

Norfolk Island, located further east in the Southern Pacific Ocean, with a similar latitude to Lismore in NSW, is home to a community of approximately 1,700 residents living amidst its lush landscapes and historical sites. Closer to New Zealand than Australia by air, this island is unique for its harmonious blend of cultures, with descendants of the Bounty mutineers and Tahitian people coexisting. Norfolk Island holds a rich history, once serving as a convict settlement during the early 19th century, a period you can explore in places like the

Kingston and Arthur's Vale Historic Area. The island also has a deep Aboriginal heritage.

The Australian Antarctic Territory (AAT), while not an island, is a vast region encompassing a portion of East Antarctica. Many countries share claims to this continent, but Australia has the largest claim. The AAT, is home to Mawson, Davis, and Casey research stations, which are staffed all year round, but have no permanent population. This territory is vital for scientific research, particularly in the areas of climate change, biology, and geology.

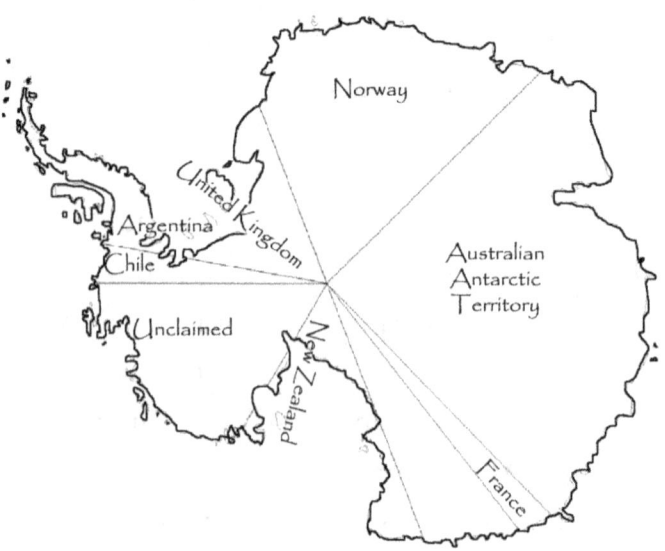

Countries with Antarctic Territorial Claims

In the Southern Ocean, about midway between Tasmania and Antarctica, is the uninhabited subantarctic island of Macquarie Island. It's known for its remarkable biodiversity, particularly its seals and penguins. The island is a World Heritage site due to its rich and unique ecosystem.

The subantarctic islands, Heard and McDonald Islands, are remote places in the Southern Ocean which are of particular interest to geologists, vulcanologists, and ecological researchers due to their active volcanoes. These uninhabited islands of fire and ice are used for study and conservation purposes.

Australia's external territories offer distinct climates, populations, and captivating stories waiting to be explored.

Discovery Activities

1. Tell what you have learnt this lesson.

2. Find these places on a map:

- Cocos (Keeling) Islands
- Christmas Island
- Ashmore and Cartier Islands
- Coral Sea Island
- Norfolk Island
- Australian Antarctic Territory
- Heard and McDonald Islands

3. Investigate an Australian external territory.

13. Our Neighbours – Indonesia

When I was twenty-seven, I went to Indonesia for a three-week holiday. On our trip we enjoyed the soft sands and crystal beaches of Bali and Lombok. We explored the Hindu temples and the mountain rice paddies of Ubud. Mischievous monkeys bombarded us whenever we were at tourist sites. They would try to eat our food or grab our camera. One morning we came out of our room to find the monkeys had gotten into our living area and stolen our fruit, leaving the skins behind.

We visited the night markets, a bustling place full of clothes, jewellery, and tourist knick-knacks. There were so many beautiful things to look at including the intricate shadow puppets used in storytelling. A golden, blue and black patchwork quilt caught our eye and we haggled to buy it and then, once we got it, we wondered how on earth we would fit it in our suitcase for the trip home.

Each day we enjoyed the local cuisine. Some of our favourites were nasi goreng (fried rice with egg and peanut sauce), satay chicken, and rendang (a tender coconut milk beef stew) and then for snacks we ate tropical fruits and pineapples on sticks.

Bali is one of the most famous beach destinations in Indonesia and is popular with Australians and New Zealanders. But there are many more places to explore in this fascinating country. Indonesia is made up of over 17,000 islands, with some of the largest being Sumatra, Java, Borneo, and Sulawesi. These islands are like pieces of a puzzle floating in the sea.

The country is part of the Ring of Fire, a circle of volcanoes. These volcanoes can sometimes erupt. The most devastating eruption was in Krakatoa in 1883. It was so loud it could be heard all the way in Australia and Mauritius, which are very far away. The explosion destroyed most of the island and caused big waves called

tsunamis. Sadly, over 30 000 people lost their lives because of this volcanic eruption.

Jakarta, Indonesia's capital, situated on the north-west coast of Java, is one of the world's most populous islands. It is a vast, bustling city with tall buildings, busy streets with cars and motorbikes, and colourful marketplaces selling delicious foods and unique objects. Although densely populated, Jakarta boasts great parks and playgrounds for youngsters and a rich history of Indonesia.

The people of Indonesia come from various backgrounds and cultures. They speak more than 700 languages, but Bahasa Indonesia and Javanese are the most common. Indonesia's main religion is Islam, and it has the largest Muslim population in the world with 85% of the people declaring themselves Muslim. However, in Bali 90% of the population are Hindu.

Indonesians wear various types of clothing based on their region. The sarong is often described as an Indonesian skirt; it is a large tube or length of fabric, often wrapped around the waist and worn by men and women throughout much of the Indonesian archipelago. Sarongs can be one of the most versatile pieces one can own.

The island of Borneo, also known as Kalimantan, is the third largest island (excluding Australia). Indonesia, Malaysia and Brunei share this island. Much of the Indonesian wood and palm oil comes from this island. However, this has come at a cost to the local wildlife as deforestation has led to the loss of their natural habitat.

New Guinea is the second largest island in the world and Indonesia shares this island with Papua New Guinea. The Indonesian portion is called Papua Western New Guinea, also known as Papua, Indonesian New Guinea, and Indonesian Papua.

There are a lot of rainforests within Indonesia which are lush, green and teeming with life. In the heart of these rainforests, you can find orangutans, large, gentle apes, that swing from tree to tree, making their homes high up in the canopy. Pygmy Elephants are found in Sumatra and Borneo and less than 200 endangered rhinos live in the Sumatran national parks. The elusive Sumatran tigers prowl here as well. These big cats are among the rarest in the world, and they move with grace and power through the dense vegetation, making them an icon of the wilderness. Their population is critically endangered and the two other tiger species from Indonesia are already extinct. Another interesting animal found in these forests is the world's smallest deer, the Mouse

Deer. These tiny, adorable creatures are no bigger than a rabbit but have long legs and a curious nature. They dart through the underbrush, blending in with the forest floor.

Indonesia is a biodiversity hotspot, which means it's filled with countless other unique and exotic animals, including colourful birds like the hornbill, playful gibbons swinging through the trees, and even the elusive and fascinating Komodo dragon, which is the world's largest lizard. The rich rainforests of Indonesia also host countless species of insects, frogs, and plants that are found nowhere else on Earth. It's a place where nature's imagination seems to have no bounds, and every corner of the forest holds a surprise waiting to be discovered. Exploring the jungles of Indonesia is like stepping into a real-life storybook of wildlife and natural wonders.

Indonesia consists of almost 18,000 islands spanning between the Pacific and Indian Oceans. It's a place to explore lush rainforests, relax on breathtaking beaches, and immerse yourself in their rich culture. Indonesia offers ancient wonders, delicious cuisine, and a wealth of creativity. Would you like to go there one day?

Discovery Activities

1. Tell what you have learnt this lesson.

2. Find these places on a map:

- Jakarta
- Bali
- Java
- Borneo
- Lombok
- Timor
- Sulawesi
- West New Guinea
- Timor Sea
- Java Sea
- South China Sea

3. Find out more about Krakatoa and the volcanoes of Indonesia.

14. Our Neighbours – Papua New Guinea

I have never been to Papua New Guinea, but my grandad told me about his time there during the Second World War. He was stationed at Krankit, a small island half an hour from Port Moresby. One side of the island was a protected lagoon surrounded by a coral reef which kept the sharks away. For thirteen months he worked at an Australian Airforce radar base. And even though it was war time, he enjoyed what he called his time on an island paradise. During that war, Papua New Guinea was considered part of Australia. It became an independent country in 1975.

Geographically, Papua New Guinea is Australia's closest neighbour, separated only by the narrow stretch of water, the Torres Strait.

There are more than 600 islands in the Independent State of Papua New Guinea, also called PNG. The main island is New Guinea. Bougainville Island and New Britain are two of the other larger islands but there are many other smaller inhabited and uninhabited islands.

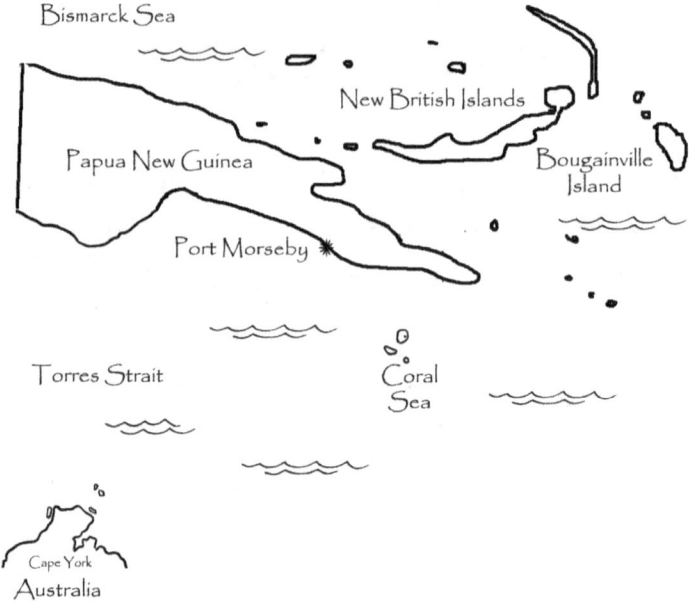

Only the eastern half of New Guinea island is part of Papua New Guinea, the western half of the island of New Guinea is part of Indonesia. This is because a long time ago, the island of New Guinea was home to many different groups of people who had their own languages and cultures. When European countries like the Netherlands and the United Kingdom started exploring and colonising different parts of the world, they arrived in this region. The Dutch colonised the western half of the island (which was called the Dutch East Indies), while the British took control of the eastern part (which was called British New Guinea). Later on, when

Indonesia and Papua New Guinea were becoming independent countries, there were agreements and negotiations about the borders. Today, this division remains, with the western part belonging to Indonesia and the eastern part to Papua New Guinea. Even though they have different governments, the people on both sides of the island share similar cultures, languages, and histories. The climate of Papua New Guinea is much like that of Indonesia.

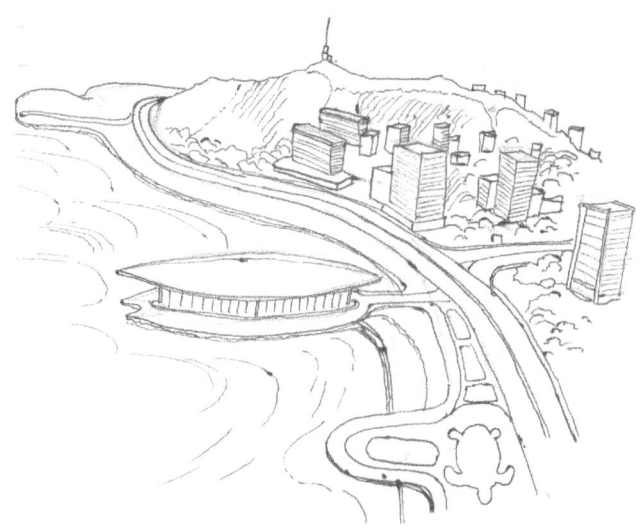

Port Moresby, often called Pom City or simply Moresby, serves as the capital and largest city of Papua New Guinea. In fact, it stands as the largest city in the South Pacific, excluding Australia and New Zealand. Nestled on the shores of the Gulf of Papua, it graces the southwestern coast of the Papuan Peninsula on the island of New Guinea. The city's origins trace back to the latter part of the 19th century when it bloomed into a thriving trade centre. During World War II, Port Moresby was very important because the Japanese wanted to use it as a base to stop ships and planes from going between Australia, Southeast Asia, and America.

Papua New Guinea is a true cultural mosaic, with over 800 different languages spoken across the country. The people of Papua New Guinea are known for their rich and diverse traditions. 96% of the people living there identify themselves as Christian. They celebrate their heritage through music, dance, and vibrant festivals. Each region has its own distinct cultural practices and art forms, from intricate wood carvings to traditional paintings and masks. Storytelling is a significant part of their culture, often conveyed through song, dance, and the art of storytelling.

The people of Papua New Guinea place high importance on community and relationships. They have a strong sense of belonging to their tribes and villages, and these social bonds are crucial for their way of life.

Mineral mining, especially gold, but also copper, silver, nickel and cobalt are Papua New Guinea's main exports.

Papua New Guinea does not have any coal mines or coal fired electricity. Instead, electricity is made from hydropower, diesel, gas and geothermal sources. It is one of the least electrified countries in the world, with only 13% of the population having access to electricity.

Cocoa is also a growing export for the people of PNG, especially in Bougainville. Prior to 2008 they were a leading producer, but then all the crops were affected by a disease and crops failed. With the help of some foreign aid (mostly from Australia), Papua New Guinea farmers are getting support to grow other crops as well, including coffee, vanilla and livestock.

The country's extensive river systems, including the Sepik River, the longest river on the island of Papua New Guinea, snake their way through the landscape, providing essential transportation and sustenance for many communities. These rivers are also rich in aquatic life and support the unique Sepik culture, where the men paddle their narrow dugout canoes ready to trade their goods and wood carvings, while the women prepare food, and the children splash and play in the river.

This country is a land of contrasts, from towering mountain ranges to lush rainforests, and breathtaking coastlines. The highlands in the central region boast some of the highest peaks in Oceania, including Mount

Wilhelm. These mountains are not only strikingly beautiful but are also home to numerous unique plant and animal species.

Papua New Guinea's dense rainforests are known for their incredible biodiversity. These jungles are teeming with a large selection of plant and animal life, including exotic birds like the Raggiana bird-of-paradise, which is featured on the national flag, as well as numerous orchid species.

Pristine beaches and coral reefs make it an underwater paradise for divers, offering a glimpse into vibrant marine life and colourful coral formations.

In this captivating land, you'll encounter a remarkable blend of modern and traditional lifestyles. While cities like Port Moresby have a more urban feel, many communities throughout the country maintain their traditional customs and live in harmony with nature.

Discovery Activities

1. Tell what you have learnt this lesson.

2. Find these places on a map:

- Papua New Guinea
- Port Moresby
- New British Islands
- Bougainville Island
- Coral Sea
- Torres Strait
- Bismarck Sea

3. Find out more about the Sepik culture.

15. Our Neighbours – South Pacific

In my early twenties, I worked as a nurse on a cruise ship that toured the South Pacific Islands. Our trip began in Sydney and then set off across the Pacific Ocean to visit Vanuatu, New Caledonia and Fiji. For the first twenty-four hours after leaving land I struggled to find my sea legs and felt very queasy, but I had to keep working because the hospital corridors were lined with people waiting to get an injection to stop their sea sickness as well. Our team of nurses must have administered nearly 1000 sea sickness injections on our first day at sea. The porters who looked after the cabins were walking around passing out bags and carrying little buckets of sand that they would throw on the piles of vomit left by some poor passenger who didn't get a bag in time.

For three sunny days we headed southeast and then we came to Port Vila, the capital of Vanuatu. It was a sleepy

town thirty-five years ago but today Port Vila has water theme parks, museums, colleges and urban sprawl. Most of the locals speak either English or French but they all speak Bislama, which is a type of pidgin English.

We hired a local taxi driver who took us around for the day to show us his island. First, we went to a local waterfall where we enjoyed swimming and jumping from small waterfalls into a deep clear waterhole. Then he took us to his village where we tried kava which is a type of drink they brew made from the root of a plant. I only had a little but it tasted like chalky muddy water.

Vanuatu is a casual place, and everyone wears t-shirts and shorts. On special occasions, men often wear colourful wraps called 'nambas', and women wear brightly coloured skirts made from grass or leaves, and sometimes they decorate their bodies with beautiful flowers and jewellery!

After a day on shore, we were back to cruising some of the smaller islands in the Pacific. When we got off the cruise ship, people went snorkelling and scuba diving in the smooth aqua waters. We were all told to be very careful of coral cuts because they often caused infections. My job at one of these island stops was to sit on the beach under an umbrella ready to treat anyone who might need first aid for a coral cut. That night we were served dinner in banana leaves and ate a South Pacific curry while the locals sang us beautiful songs and performed their traditional dances.

Our next stop on the ship was New Caledonia, an overseas territory of France located in the South Pacific. Most of the population in New Caledonia is of Melanesian descent, and the territory has a unique blend of French and Melanesian cultures. We visited two of the smaller islands and then went to Nouméa, the capital. I'd been told to expect a Parisian shopping experience but when we finally got there it was lunchtime, and all the shops were shut because they have a siesta from 11am to 2pm every day. To kill time, we went and ate lunch, but our options were limited because of the siesta, and we paid tourist prices for our meals which were ten times more than the local price. A coke was $10 and that was more than 35 years ago. When the shops finally opened, I was tempted and bought a shiny emerald-green designer label top which I wore for many years after that.

Some islands in Fiji were also part of the cruise and each port was one beautiful place after another. But when we got to Suva it was different. The Fijian capital was very busy and there was a strong military presence at the port. Soldiers stood with guns watching us get on board and it was a little scary. The shopping was good, and I was surprised at how many people were of Indian descent—about 35% of the population are Indo-Fijian.

After fourteen days cruising, we finished our cruise but most of the time, unless you looked on a map, you would not know what country you were in. While it's challenging to give an exact count, there are approximately 2,000 to 2,500 islands in the Melanesian region. Some of the more well-known and larger islands in this region include Papua New Guinea, Fiji, Solomon Islands, Vanuatu, and New Caledonia. These islands are part of the larger group of islands that make up the Melanesian region. Most communities live a rural village lifestyle and share traditions and many of these islands have no inhabitants.

Tourism is a source of income for lots of these countries, but did you know the climate is also excellent for growing chocolate trees. That's not technically right, they actually grow cacao trees and from these trees we get cocoa which is the raw ingredient used to make chocolate. The Pacific Island countries of Fiji, Samoa, Solomon Islands, and Vanuatu all export a lot of cocoa. In Vanuatu, 25% of rural households are involved in cocoa production, and in the Solomon Islands, cocoa is the most valuable agricultural export, bringing in about $20 million per year.

Discovery Activities

1. Tell what you have learnt this lesson.

2. Find these places on a map:

- Fiji
- Suva
- New Caledonia
- Noumea
- Vanuatu
- Port Vila

2. Find 5 other island nations in the South Pacific region.

16. Our Neighbours – New Zealand

On my most recent visit to New Zealand we flew into Christchurch, the largest city in the South Island. It was summer and I went there with my family. Being closer to the South Pole than Tasmania, the temperature was cool, and we often had our jumpers on. Daylight lasted for 15 hours, and sunset was not till 9pm at night.

The Ōtākaro/Avon River starts at Avonhead and runs through the heart of Christchurch City and suburbs, then it empties out into the Pacific Ocean. There is a charming story about an elephant seal, affectionately called Elisabeth by the locals, who lived in the river. She sometimes shocked visitors when they saw her sunbathing on the riverbank. There was once an attempt to take her back to her sub-Antarctic home, but she returned shortly after. For nearly 20 years she lived in the river until she died in 1985.

Christchurch reminds you of a European city. There are boats punting along the river, like you see in Venice, Italy. Many bridges and buildings have European architecture, the trees and flowers remind you of England. The Botanic Gardens were the highlight of the city. The rose garden was in full bloom and we stopped to smell the fragrance of many of them. Christchurch is prone to earthquakes, and you can still see evidence of this with their historic Christchurch Cathedral, still unrepaired since the 2011 damage. In order to provide a place for worshippers the Cardboard Cathedral was built. This innovative structure is an A frame design made with cardboard tubes, a polycarbonate roof and shipping containers for walls. The foundation is a concrete slab.

After three days in Christchurch it was time to leave. Unfortunately, we didn't have time to visit New Zealand's southernmost cities, Queenstown, and Dunedin (a town with a strong Scottish heritage). However, friends of mine have been and say the walk along the Milford Track to Milford Sound (a fiord) is 'the finest walk in the world'. Winter and summer sports are popular in this region. The ski fields are popular worldwide for people who want to hit the slopes from June to October. We decided we'll go there on our next New Zealand holiday.

From Christchurch, the next part of our journey was through the valley of Arthur's Pass which was surrounded by majestic mountains, still with snow on their tips. We stopped here to look at some of the locations where the *Lord of the Rings* was filmed.

That night we stayed in Otira at a very quirky hotel filled with odd curiosities; taxidermy possums holding guns were on one side of the dining room, creepy clay circus clown heads decorated the other side, a collection of hand painted porcelain toilet bowls lined the corridor, and a massive statue of Golem stood tall in the carpark. Even dinner was unusual. After eating rich greasy food for the last few meals, I decided that night would be a good night for a salad—but I was wrong—I was given over-ripe soggy tomato, detergent tasting lettuce, and frozen grated cheese. My children assured me that the chips and burger were the better choice. The saving grace of that hotel was just how weird it really was, and even though the lock broke in our room, and we had to yell out for someone to release us—we were not fazed. The Otira Stagecoach Hotel is now etched in our memory.

From Otira we continued west to Greymouth, then north through valleys of Marlborough, New Zealand's wine region where I saw some of the most picturesque lush green mountains I have ever seen. It was unexpectedly breathtaking. We arrived in Picton, an adorable place that stole our hearts. It's perched at the top of the South Island, surrounded by lush green hills and overlooking the stunning Queen Charlotte Sound. Quaint stores, cafes, and art galleries contribute to its small-town charm as you stroll its quiet streets. Friendly residents, colourful flowers, and a picturesque shoreline where you can watch ferries are the town's hallmarks.

After a day sightseeing, we caught the ferry to the North Island. As we departed from the South Island, we crossed the picturesque Cook Strait, which was quite windy and wavy that day.

After a few hours we were docking in the deep harbour of Wellington, a city surrounded by hills. We got off the ferry, along with the other 1,500 passengers who had done the trip with us. Dragging our suitcases we walked through the streets to the nearby hotel, which was close to the Beehive, an eye-catching government building in the nation's capital which looks like, you guessed it, a beehive!

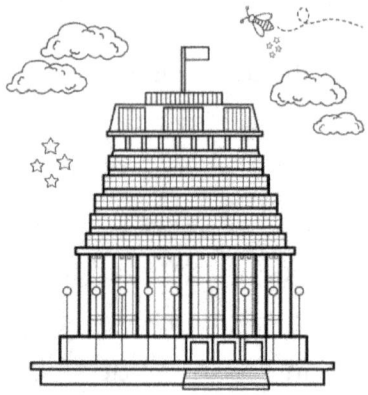

We only had one day to sightsee, so we decided to catch the iconic Wellington Cable Car up to the Botanic Gardens to get a bird's eye view of the city and its harbour. It was beautiful. That night we strolled along a waterfront packed with locals waiting for the midnight fireworks. It was New Year's Eve.

Our next stop was Lake Taupo. The whole area is known for its volcanic activity, and it smells like rotten eggs—all the time, which technically is caused by the sulfuric gasses coming from all the geothermal activity. One of my children wanted to go Bungy jumping but he couldn't convince the rest of us. After picking him out of the river after his big drop, we went back to our accommodation and enjoyed a soak in the thermal pool in our hotel.

Back in the car the next morning, we headed to Rotorua in the middle of the North Island. A place that also had that rotten egg smell. We spent our time there sightseeing Māori culture and visiting the bubbling mud pools, local forest, and looking at geysers blowing steam and water high into the sky. This was not my first time to this thermal wonderland; my parents had taken me there when I was six years old. My mother took my sister and I for a 'relaxing soak' in one of the hot springs, but the heat was too much for me, I boiled over and fainted and I spent the rest of the day in bed – which was a shame because it was Christmas day.

From Rotorua we went to Hobbiton. We were looking forward to this because it was like stepping into a magical world from *The Lord of the Rings* and *The Hobbit* movies. The tiny hobbit houses and lush, green hills make you feel like you're in the heart of the Shire. It's an enchanting place where you can see where your favourite Hobbiton characters lived and enjoy the stunning countryside.

From there we went to the Coromandel Coast on the Eastern coast of the North Island. We stayed near Hot

Water Beach, a place where you can dig your own hot pools in the sand. We saw lots of people with spades, but no hot pools. The next day we hiked down to the stunning beach at Cathedral Cove. This area served as the backdrop for the Pevensie children's return to Narnia in the movie Prince Caspian. Of course my children reenacted the scene.

We didn't visit the Bay of Islands in the North on this trip, but I had been there before. It is both an historic and beautiful place. Here the 1840 Treaty of Waitangi, was signed by the British Crown Government and 540 Māori leaders. The gorgeous harbour town of Russell was also worth a visit with its historic buildings, cafes, arts and crafts. This European settlement seaport retains its 1843 street layout and names. You can go on a short boat excursion to the northern tip and observe numerous spectacular rock sculptures made by years of ocean waves. On one of these trips several of us felt queasy, so the personnel gave us roast chicken silver foil bags in case we were sick. Apparently, they had run out of seasick bags. Luckily, most of us returned home with empty chicken bags.

Our trip to New Zealand was nearly over. So we had to leave the west side of the Northern Island unexplored which was a shame because I really wanted to visit

Waitomo Glowworm Caves, but it was time to head home.

After spending a night in Auckland, the largest city in New Zealand, we hopped on a plane and three hours later we were back in Sydney, my home Down Under.

Discovery Activities

1. Tell what you have learnt this lesson.

2. Find these places on a map:

- South Island
- Christchurch
- Queenstown
- Dunedin
- Arthur's Pass
- Cook's Strait
- North Island
- Wellington
- Taupo
- Rotorua
- Auckland
- Bay of Islands

3. Plan your own trip around New Zealand. Mark out the places you would like to visit.